A+ books

WORLD OF COLORS

Brazil in Colors

by Ann Stalcup

Consultant: Colin M. MacLachlan
John Christy Barr
Distinguished Professor of History
Tulane University
New Orleans, Louisiana

Capstone press
Mankato, Minnesota

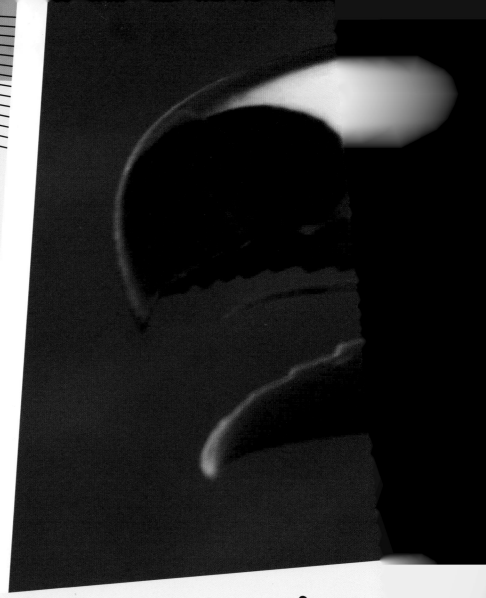

Black and **white** toucans hop from branch to branch in Brazil's rain forests. They use their long **orange** beaks to pick berries from trees. Toucans also eat insects, lizards, and small birds.

The **white** water of Iguassu Falls crashes onto the rocks in southwestern Brazil. The falls stretch for 2 miles (3.2 kilometers) along the border of Brazil and Argentina. Visitors admire the 275 small waterfalls that make up Iguassu.

Members of the Kayapó tribe wear **red**, **blue**, and **yellow** beads. The Kayapó live in central Brazil. They grow crops like sweet potatoes and fruit. The Kayapó also hunt, fish, and gather seeds and berries. Brazil is home to about 215 American Indian tribes.

A farmer rounds up his herd of **white** beef cattle. Cattle ranches are found on the rich grasslands of southern Brazil. Brazil is a world leader in producing beef.

Red *feijoada* is Brazil's national dish. Feijoada is a stew made from black beans, meat, and spices. Brazilians eat the stew with orange slices, rice, and kale.

Green water lilies float on the Amazon River in northern Brazil. The Amazon is the world's second-longest river. But it carries more water than any other river on earth.

Brown Brazil nuts grow in Brazil's northern forests. Workers gather the nuts from trees that grow near the Amazon River. The nuts are then sold to other countries.

Visitors from around the world enjoy Rio de Janeiro's **blue** water and **white** sandy beaches. Rio is the second-largest city in Brazil. It is also an important port on the Atlantic Ocean.

Green tree boas sleep curled on leafy branches. Tree boas live along the Amazon River. They grow up to 6 feet (1.8 meters) long. Tree boas eat mice, rats, and other small animals. They squeeze prey to death and swallow it whole.

Brazilian kids play soccer on a **blue** and **white** plaza. Soccer is Brazil's most popular sport. Brazil's soccer team has won the World Cup five times.

Blue and **yellow** apartment buildings tower over a busy city street in Brazil. Most Brazilians live in cities. Grandparents, parents, and children sometimes share the same home.

A **golden** float dazzles the crowd during a Carnival parade in Rio de Janeiro. Carnival is a festival. It lasts for four days and nights before the start of Lent. Visitors from around the world come to Brazil to celebrate Carnival.

A samba dancer performs in a **purple** costume. Samba is a popular dance in Brazil. Samba is fast, bouncy, and joyful. Brazil has many samba schools. The schools practice all year to perform in Rio's Carnival parade. They compete for the prize of best samba school.

FACTS about Brazil

Capital City: Brasília

Population: 196,342,592

Official Language: Portuguese

Common Phrases

English	Portuguese	Pronunciation
hello	oi	(OY)
good-bye	tchau	(CHOW)
yes	sim	(SEEM)
no	não	(NOU)

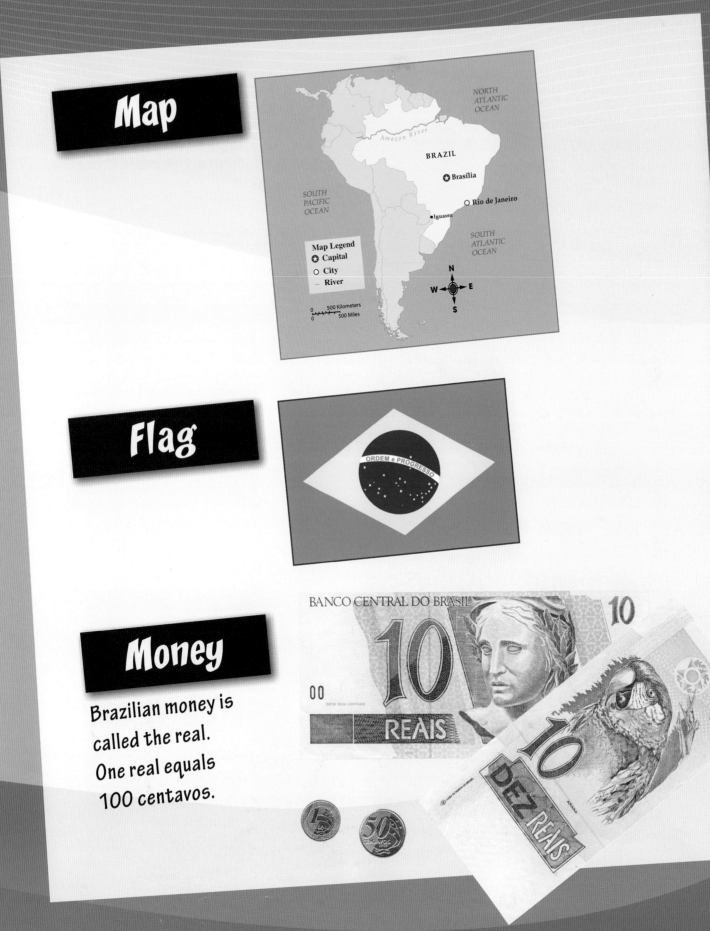

Map

Flag

Money

Brazilian money is called the real. One real equals 100 centavos.

Glossary

Carnival (KAHR-nuh-vuhl) — a festival celebrated before the Christian period of Lent; Lent is the 40 days before Easter.

feijoada (fay-joh-AH-duh) — a type of stew made from black beans and meat

festival (FES-tuh-vuhl) — a celebration that is held at the same time each year

kale (KALE) — a type of cabbage

Kayapó (kah-yuh-POH) — a member of an American Indian people who lives in central Brazil

port (PORT) — a harbor where ships dock safely

rain forest (RAYN FOR-ist) — a thick forest where a great deal of rain falls

samba (SAHM-bah) — Brazilian music with a heavy beat; samba is also a type of dance.

toucan (TOO-kan) — a brightly colored tropical bird that has a very large beak

World Cup (WURLD CUP) — a soccer competition held every four years in a different country; teams from around the world compete against each other; Brazil has won the World Cup more times than any other country.

Read More

Bauer, Brandy. *Brazil. Questions and Answers. Countries.* Mankato, Minn.: Capstone Press, 2005.

Seidman, David. *Brazil ABCs: A Book about the People and Places of Brazil. Country ABCs.* Minneapolis: Picture Window Books, 2007.

Internet Sites

FactHound offers a safe, fun way to find educator-approved Internet sites related to this book.

Here's what you do:

1. Visit www.facthound.com

2. Choose your grade level.

3. Begin your search.

This book's ID number is 9781429622226.

FactHound will fetch the best sites for you!

Index

A+ Books are published by Capstone Press,
151 Good Counsel Drive, P.O. Box 669, Mankato, Minnesota 56002.
www.capstonepress.com

1 2 3 4 5 6 14 13 12 11 10 09

Library of Congress Cataloging-in-Publication Data
Stalcup, Ann, 1935–
  Brazil in colors / by Ann Stalcup.
    p. cm. — (A+ books. World of colors)
  Includes bibliographical references and index.
  Summary: "Simple text and striking photographs present Brazil, its culture,
and its geography" — Provided by publisher.
    ISBN-13: 978-1-4296-2222-6 (hardcover)
    ISBN-10: 1-4296-2222-9 (hardcover)
  1. Brazil — Juvenile literature. I. Title. II. Series.
F2508.5.S73 2009   2008034122
981 — dc22

Credits

Megan Peterson, editor; Veronica Bianchini, set designer; Kyle Grenz, book designer;
    Wanda Winch, photo researcher

Photo Credits

Alamy/Sue Cunningham Photographic, 6–7; Alamy/travelstock44, 27; Art Life
Images/Juan Carlos Munoz, 12–13; Art Life Images/OSOMEDIA, 20; Banco Centro
do Brasil, 29 (coins); Capstone Press/Karon Dubke, 14; iStockphoto/Jed Shein, cover;
Shutterstock/Celso Pupo, 16–17; Shutterstock/Eduardo Rivero, 4–5; Shutterstock/
Hannamariah, 18–19; Shutterstock/Imagemaker, 2–3; Shutterstock/Maria Weidner, 1;
Shutterstock/Mityukhin Oleg Petrovich, 29 (banknotes); Shutterstock/Tristan Quesnelle
29 (flag); South American Pictures/Marion Morrison, 24–25; South American Pictures/
Tony Morrison, 8–9, 10–11, 22–23

Note to Parents, Teachers, and Librarians

This World of Colors book uses full-color photographs and a nonfiction format
to introduce children to basic topics in the study of countries. *Brazil in Colors*
is designed to be read aloud to a pre-reader or to be read independently by an
early reader. Photographs help listeners and early readers understand the text
and concepts discussed. The book encourages further learning by including the
following sections: Facts about Brazil, Glossary, Read More, Internet Sites, and
Index. Early readers may need assistance using these features.